**Chica E. Casey**

INSPIRING AUTHOR

**Disclaimer Notice: The Information in this book is based on my life experiences and is in no way a duplicate of someone else's work. Any resemblances of any kind are merely coincidental.**



Chica Casey/Chica & The Family Produktionz
chicaandthefamilyproduktionz@outlook.com

**Edited by: Cynthia Murray**

**Library of Congress
Cataloging in Publication Data**

**ISBN 978-0-9816509-0-6**

**Printed in the U.S.A**

**All scriptures were referenced from the NIV Study Bible.**

# “Babe in Christ”

**Growing while walking with the Lord**

## BY

## Chica E. Casey

“A word to the wise”

Don’t try to figure out what God is doing in your life just let go and let God!

“Trust in the Lord with all thine heart and lean not to thine own understanding. In all thy ways acknowledge him and he shall direct thy paths.”
**Proverbs 3:5-6 NIV Study Bible**

In the mist of my storms **JESUS** kept me warm!

# "Babe in Christ"

Growing while walking with the Lord

A book of short stories, statements of opinion, testimonies, prayers and poetry relating to experiences that I've endured in life. I had to overcome the fear of failing, rejection, lack of love, intense pain and a divorce. It expresses how I have grown through these experiences while walking with the Lord. It has given me peace and stability, grounded on a solid foundation for me to move forward in the most positive way. To achieve the goals that God has set for me in life. This is to bring out the best in me for someone else. I'm blessed to be a blessing.

I have embraced the truths in my heart. I have decided not to hide them or to pretend that it doesn't hurt me anymore. Instead, I will face and heal from all that I endure in life. I have been on what I would call an emotional rollercoaster, going in and out of hell for several years, where I don't want my life to end. I am finally free to be all that God has created me to be.

The most important thing to me in writing this book is to encourage women all over the world to break free from their past. To help young ladies deal with their issues at an early age so that they won't linger on into their adulthood and for young men to appreciate what it takes to be a young lady and respect those boundaries.

***STEP UP TO HEALING. IT'S A PROCESS !***

**Special thanks to my family:**
**Brandon, Landon and Brandon Jr. Crutchfield.**
**Briana, Rico, and Delmarius Stith.**
**Susan D. Temple and to all of my family that I did not mention. I LOVE YOU!**

**To: My favorite cousin Andre Casey (Big Dray), who is more like a brother to me and who always looks out for me (no questions asked). You've never asked for anything in return. I know that everything you do is from the heart. I love you little bro. Thank you for keeping it real 4-life.**

**To: Mr. E, all that you've done to try and bring me down, God turned it unto good. I forgive you. Thanks. I'm more than a conqueror!**

## Concepts

### "Just a babe"

when you choose to serve God, the devil comes immediately to distract you. You have to keep your faith in God to heal you in your situations then you'll see how awesome he is, as you use the power of prayer.

### "Getting to know God"

By getting to know God we learn that it is a process therefore it will take time. We won't change overnight. We have to walk with him and be obedient to his will. Know that test and trials will come but with God we can surely declare the victory because the battle is not ours it's the Lords.

### "My Vision"

The way I see my life now and how it encourages me to push harder to receive and fulfill my purpose as God wants me to do.

### "Jesus you are the love of my life"

Expresses how grateful I am to God for showing me love. Now I don't feel needy anymore.

### "Now I know why she couldn't love me unconditionally"

Reveals how a woman who has been hurt and rejected at times in her life held on to her pain therefore she couldn't show love to her daughter that she desperately needed.

## God help me to understand and redeem my self-esteem"

Describes how I had so many dreams growing up. I got married at an early age only to end up divorced. My self-esteem was lowered and all I could do was cry out to God for help.

## "Is he the one?"

Expresses how I have been waiting on God to bless me with a good man at heart. One who would love and respect me as God's Word has commanded and who has a willing heart because that's something God can work with.

## "Life is like a jigsaw puzzle"

My opinion about how life can be so mind boggling at times but in all that we go through, we must learn how to trust God because he knows what he is doing and what's best for us. We can't predict our future but God will guide us if we let him.

# Table of Contents

# “Just a babe”

# "Just a babe"
## Scenario One: The Distractions

You see, as a young girl I had a will in my heart to serve God, but I just didn't know how. As I grew older, at times I would pray to God and ask him what was wrong with me, why I didn't feel saved like other people (being that I had been baptized)? When I would go to church, my mind was so focused on other people that were in the church, that I could not see my purpose for being there in the first place. "I mean I was messed up". I worried about how people were looking at me. I would be afraid to go to the altar for prayer just because I thought others would judge me. I felt like I had butterflies in my stomach.

I would stand still and grieve the Holy Spirit. I would go to other churches trying to find my rightful place and if I didn't feel comfortable, off to another church I went. My life kept getting harder. Tests and trials would come my way and I asked God why? I would say Lord; "You know my heart so why haven't I changed yet"? It seemed to me that I could not get an answer, so I would go on with my life as it was. I would forget to pray. I thought that the world had a lot to offer me, if I would only work hard enough to get it. When times were tough, I would only call on God in my time of need. When things went the way I wanted them to, I would get happy and forget to thank God. If they did not go my way, I would again ask the Lord why? "I was so selfish" and for a long time I went through several tests and was ashamed to acknowledge it. Praying was the only thing that kept me going. As I matured, my will to serve God grew stronger. I was still weak even more than I knew. I would see and talk to people that was into the Word and it would touch my heart. I had a very good friend that would talk about the Lord and I could see the anointing upon her.

She had such a beautiful heart and will to serve God. It sent chills through my body when we talked about how God was dealing with her and I prayed for the Holy Spirit to use me. I began to seek God and hungered for his Word. Although I continued to backslide, I did not give up. I still did not understand why I wasn't changing the way I lived my life. I went through a stage where all I wanted to do was read my bible. I read three times a day, everyday for about four months. I did not want anyone around me that was not carrying on a conversation about the mercy of God.

One day another dear friend of mine who was changing her life for the Lord, asked me to go to church with her and for a while, I kept making excuses why I could not go. All of a sudden I had this overwhelming urge to go, so I went with her to church that very next Sunday. Service was so anointed by the presence of the Holy Spirit; it really touched my heart. I felt like I wanted to join the church so I did. You know Satan was angry then. He kept sending people my way to confuse me. I was so puzzled that all I could do was doubt.

He made me think twice about my decision to join that blessed church. I called the Pastor the next day and told him that I did not feel comfortable about joining the church at that time. He asked me who had I been talking to and I told him no one (I lied). I allowed others to distract me. After taking back my membership, I still continued to seek God's Word. I decided to go back to the church I grew up in. I could not understand what the Pastor was saying and I surely didn't know if what he was saying had anything to do with me living my life the way God wanted me to.

Things were even more confusing. Late that evening when I arrived home from church, I fell on my bed and cried. I prayed to God for guidance. I wanted to know if taking back my membership was the right thing to do. Immediately after I had finished praying a peace came over me. I opened my bible and the Holy Spirit guided me to the book of Romans. Everything I had been questioning, the Lord showed me the answer. I felt so relieved. My faith was lifted, but I still had not gone back to the church for a while.

I went from reading my bible three times a day to every other day and then once a week. I felt bad, as if I was neglecting the Lord. I told my friend and she suggested that I pray to God about it (in my mind I didn't know how to pray). Also if I could not remember what to say, to write the prayer down and then pray, but as you probably already know satan still had his hand on me. He tried to convince me that I didn't need to write the prayer down. Two days later the Holy Spirit kept putting it on my heart to write down everything I wanted to make a change in, what I was worried about and pray on it, so I did.

He told me to ask for forgiveness in Jesus name, name the problem, claim deliverance from those things and thank God for delivering me from them. I went back to the church I had withdrawn my membership from and I rejoined. It felt good. My faith was a little stronger but I still could not see my life changing so I continued to read the prayer. One night Satan was telling me that I was too tired to pray. The Holy Spirit on the other hand told me to pray anyway. It was a Friday night I will never forget. I went to sleep after prayer and at 2:30 a.m. that Saturday morning, I woke up and could not go back to sleep for nothing.

I was tossing and turning; I could not keep my mind off of the Lord. The Holy Spirit instructed me. Get up and write this down, he said, but satan was telling me that I was too tired and sleepy to write. The Holy Spirit would not let go. Again he said, get up and write this down. I got up and started writing. I began to question what the Holy Spirit was telling me to write. He stopped me and said don't worry about it, just keep writing. I was writing so fast that I did not stop to see if what I was writing made any sense or if it was spelled correctly. Then the Holy Spirit instructed me to read it and this is what it said:

## "Words from the Holy Spirit"

I believe in God, I love God, I have faith in God, I trust in God, and I am saved! Teach me to be righteous and may my cup be filled. The Holy Spirit is my guide, Jesus is my savior, God is my father, and I'm blessed! There is no room for satan. He is banned from my life! I no longer belong to him. I am my father's child! I can be obedient! I am strong! The Lord is my Shepherd, I shall not want. My husband and children are saved and they are blessed. Oh, what a righteous household we have prepared, thanks to our Lord, Jesus Christ, for the Holy Spirit to dwell within.

After I had finished reading it, the Holy Spirit began to explain what it meant. Earlier I mentioned that I would pray and ask God what was wrong with me, why I wasn't changing the way I lived my life. The Holy Spirit told me that Satan had fooled me, he made me think that I could never change and be a child of God, as he knew that this was a fear I had for many years. You see it wasn't about me; it was about God he had to be the one to change me I just had to be the willing vessel. I didn't know what was going on at the time, but the Holy Spirit brought it to light and told me that Satan is a liar.

The words he had told me to write down he explained, at the beginning, this is where you are now and this is where you are going. I just had to be patient and keep fighting (the good fight of faith; that is). It was not my time then. I began to cry and shout thank you Jesus! For, answering my prayer. My life is changing now that I am saved. I see everything with a spiritual eye. Isn't God good? I can't keep my mind off of the Lord. Thank you Jesus! Now I'm beginning to understand.

## "I'm beginning to understand"

I'm beginning to understand why my life

has been up and down not seeking God first,

kept my face full of frowns. I'm slowly

making changes, but only in his name.

Christ Jesus died for me and I don't want

him to be ashamed. I have setbacks every

now and then but I don't give up because he

died for my sins. I pray and pray for the

Lord to take me in to come into my life and

never let go making me his friend forever

so that our relationship will grow. I'm

beginning to understand why my life has

been up and down. I'm beginning to

understand and now I don't have to frown.

## "Just a babe continues"

### Scenario Two: His healing hands

Today I went to church and the Holy Spirit was moving about. I learned that God wants us to have things while we are here on earth because the earth is God's, he just doesn't want those things to control us. I am being taught things that I had no idea existed and I could never see with a worldly eye. God is so mighty and great, and just when you think you know it all or you have learned everything that there is to learn, he starts working in ways we never could imagine. This is what God is doing for me.

I can't speak for anyone else but I know that I am being fed the word of God because, before I would go to church and couldn't understand anything and I really was wishing that church would hurry up and end. Now things have changed. There's no way in the world I could be a child of God, see everything with a spiritual eye, have the Holy Spirit constantly moving in my life, growing up in the word everyday and want to turn back to ungodliness. There's no way possible. I don't know everything, but I do know that God gives me the knowledge through his word to know him better.

No I'm not perfect but I'm trying my best and all God wants is my best. He will take care of the rest. Thank you Jesus! I also learned that you can believe in God and have faith in him but you have to put that faith into action, step out on it without a doubt. I knew that this message was for me, because I believed and I had faith but I didn't know what to do with it. For three weeks I had been writing down my prayers to God. Whatever I would pray about the Pastor would end up teaching on it in service. You know that is nothing but the Holy Spirit bringing forth confirmation.

I had been in so much pain in my legs and both feet for a long time. The doctor told me that I had a foot disorder and gave me information explaining what the problem was and the choices that I had for therapy. He said I could do certain exercises, which wouldn't stop the pain, but it would ease it or I could have surgery in which there were no guarantees there either. I was not having any surgery and I was tired of the exercises because as he said, it only eased the pain a little. I started praying to God about my condition off and on for about three or four weeks and I left it alone.

One Sunday I was in church and the Pastor said that someone had a condition just like mine and I never told him or anyone else in church besides God about my condition. He went on to say that the Holy Spirit told him that the Lord said it was already done. I was already healed. I received that word for my life and later on in the middle of the night, I woke up and started praying to God telling him what the Pastor had said in church that day and I claimed it.

Do you know that the next morning when I got up out of bed I could walk across the floor like I had brand new legs and feet? I was so happy. I started thanking Jesus. I had to sit on the edge of the bed for a minute and in tears I gave him praise, I just thanked him over and over. Immediately after prayer and thanking God, I went to tell my husband.

**Scenario Three: <u>The power of prayer</u>**

One day my husband was on the phone talking to a woman from his job. She wanted to know what was said about her over the phone the night before. My husband began to talk to this person and it disturbed me. I started thinking it was nothing but the devil trying to move his way in my household again. I asked my husband could I use the phone to get him off of it but he said in a minute and continued to talk. Well, I was determined that the devil was not staying in my house so; I closed my eyes and prayed to God for the conversation to end. Before I opened my eyes I could hear my husband saying alright and when I had opened them he said good-bye to the woman. That is what the power of prayer can do. I am proud to say God has been so supernaturally good to me (as well as naturally) that at times all I can do is cry tears of joy.

**Opinion**-You see, sometimes what seems to be an innocent conversation opens the door for satan to have his way. Believe me. He will use it to the fullest extent, for his advantage and our disadvantage.

"He who guards his mouth and his tongue keeps himself from calamity." **Proverbs 21:23 NIV Study Bible**

## “Grateful tears”

I cry tears of joy- grateful tears

I cry tears of appreciation- grateful tears

I cry tears cause God is good- grateful tears

My cup is running over, I cry- grateful tears

When I hear his name, I cry- grateful tears

When I’m in my home, I cry- grateful tears

He stands by my side, I cry- grateful tears

He strengthened me in my spiritual journey,

I cried- grateful tears

He opened my eyes, I cried- grateful tears

All the tears I cry are grateful tears

# “Getting to know God”

## "Getting to know God"

### The Process

It's a process and as you probably already know, God deals with us all in his own way. This is what happened to me. The **first step** is to stay focused (keep your eyes on the Lord). I don't care what the devil has placed at your feet; you can kick it out of the way, just keep your eyes on the Lord.

**Step two;** This is your refining process. Have faith and believe (give your situation to God and leave it there) it won't be easy, but go on with your life knowing that God has already taken care of things according to his will, but in your best interest.

**Step three;** Renewing of the mind (through daily bible reading, fellowship with God and applying these Godly principles to your life daily). Begin to speak the word on your life (this is putting faith into action).

**Step four;** Pray. Daily prayer is a must. You need it to live day by day whether you think you do or not.

**Step five;** If you're really serious about getting to know God, fasting and prayer together will get you a lot closer to him. Try these steps and watch how awesome God is. Don't forget to give him all the glory and the praise that he so greatly deserves.

## “Getting to know God”
### The Walk

I am being led to a pathway, through a small gate, down a straight and narrow road that leads to eternal life. In the midst of my journey, I ran into several stones. Some big, some small, but all are too heavy for me to move alone. I look around to find help. I call out for answers but no one is there. So I bow down on my knees in hope that if I just push a little harder, they will all move on their own. As I push and I push, nothing happens. I began to get worried but I kept on pushing. I cry out in tears pouring my heart out over the stones. Finally, I am almost out of breath. I hear a voice, deep but gentle and compassionate. My child he says; I’ve watched you push on those stones for a while now. You must surrender and give it up to me, for this is my job and no one else can do it but me. I will remove the stones for you but you have to follow me. Seek my face and I will take you to a place where the stones can automatically be removed. It sounded like a great plan to me so I agreed to go along. Wait I’m not finished, the Lord said; this is no ordinary place. There are some rules that you will have to follow and they can only be found by seeking my face. Alright I replied; but what if I get lost on the way? Then use your protection, which is thy word, in it you will find safe pasture.

## "Getting to know God"

### The Test

For many years everything in my life revolved around me trying to make my husband and children happy first and God last. In the process I lost my identity and didn't even know it. Now don't get me wrong, I don't regret wanting to make my loved ones happy, I do regret not putting God first. It was like an addiction for me. I wasn't happy unless they were happy and I really felt the need to make that my first priority. At one particular time in my life I felt that my whole life was tumbling down. My marriage was falling apart and I had so many questions.

My children seemed to be more disobedient and I didn't know what I was going to do. The pain was so unbearable that all I could do was cry out to God. Oh how I longed to be whole. I would say Lord, please take this pain away. I can't take it anymore. I felt like I was dying inside. It was then that I began to have an intimate relationship with God. I felt an intense need to be closer to him. Day by day, hour-by-hour, minute-by-minute, I wanted to be with no one but God. Reading my bible became an addiction and a great one if I may add. I found a greater need in my life, one that I could allow God to nurture as I began to heal (slowly). The Lord had placed a song on my heart to sing in my time of distress (Lord prepare me to be a sanctuary, pure and holy, tried and true, with thanksgiving, I'll be a living sanctuary for you). Every time I felt down, hurt or as though I couldn't make it, I would sing this song. It helped me reach another level in my healing process. Each day I grew a little stronger, God began to reveal to me my future but it was up to me to have faith and believe. At times I would be so happy that I would reveal to others some of my intimate conversations with God. They listened to me and said that they believed me and would even give their advice.

It helped to talk about the situation at the time but the Holy Spirit told me not to reveal anymore of our intimate conversations because some people may not believe and it would only distract my faith. Some conversations are to be left between you and God. That's why they are called intimate. From that point on I kept my conversations with my father to myself (unless I was lead by the Holy Spirit to be a blessing to someone else). My children and I would gather in a circle and say a family prayer for our home and our life daily. One morning I woke up and prayed my warfare prayer as I did every morning. When I finished, I began to straighten up the house.

As I walked into my bathroom the Holy Spirit had put it on my heart to sing another song (Anointing fall on me, let the power of the Holy Ghost fall on me, anointing fall on me). In a matter of seconds the Holy Spirit came over me, moved my body back and forth, side to side, and then around and around. My feet were the only part of my body that would not move. Suddenly I realized what was happening to me. It was the start of me becoming whole. God was building a sanctuary in me, so that no matter what came my way I would be rooted and grounded, still standing with him in the end. PRAISE GOD!!!

## "Getting to know God"
### The Victory

Getting to know God is the most personal, intimate relationship I have ever experienced. There is no other who can compare to the unconditional love of God. It's like having intercourse and when you reach that point of release you are set free. Intimately (with man) you feel so good, as if you could take off and fly, but only for that moment. Ha! When you have intercourse with God the relationship is much deeper than that. It feels so much greater and more powerful.

It never lacks; it totally sets you free. You are enlightened to who you really are and how precious you are to him. You recognize that you have no need to be desperate for anyone or anything but him. In relationships a desperate need for another person is only a handicap, a crutch. God should be the only one you need in that way, after all it was God who said that he would supply all of your needs according to his riches and glory by Christ Jesus (Philippians 4:19). If you can relate to this, examine yourself and give it up to God.

Make him first in everything you do (Matthew 6:33). Talk to him and ask for guidance, then listen and wait. He will direct your paths (Proverbs 3: 5-6). Your plans will be a lot easier and most successful. Now there is nothing wrong with loving and wanting to be with someone. You should want to seek God for the relationship he has ordained. All things are subject to change. Now remember that Satan is the master of manipulation.

What your flesh craves appears to look and feel real good, only to deny you of your blessings. Allow God to set your house on a solid foundation. At this point nothing by any means can tear it down. I remember when I was going through. I developed a relationship with God and would seek him through prayer, but not always quick to read his word. Therefore, it became a hindrance to my spiritual growth. I would pray for my home to be built on a solid foundation where my husband would be the head and not the tail.

I didn't want to go through the heartache and pain that it would take to get there, so that I would become solid, steadfast, fixed and immovable. I had to become faithful and even that was hard for me to do. The challenge came from within and I didn't know where to begin. As I continued to press on, God began to shine light where darkness had taken a lot out of me. I was so tired and stressed out, but my faith and strength was uplifted by his total grace and mercy.

You see there are reasons and seasons for everything you go through. I can assure you that receiving the victory in Jesus name, at the end of every obstacle is my goal.

## "Holy Spirit inspired"

I can hear the rain falling

I can see the clouds smiling

I can taste the butter that melts within

I feel the angels breathing down my neck

I see their faces

I see opened doors

I hear clouds roaring for the angel's

Appearance such a loud noise

A noise filled with mercy and grace

A cloud filled with love and his face

I see a rich man walking

I see a blind man talking

I see what you don't see

I see victory in its defeat

I see my angel in the cloud

I see victory at my feet

It's all above and not beneath

I see a soul searching in its great relief

He is the master of the universe

He is the great I am

He is my healer

He is my problem solver

He is the great I am

There is no lack in him

There is no lack in me

For my eyes have seen so much grief

It's time now for our hearts to be fulfilled

It's time now to admit that Jesus is real

I can't say enough and I'm so full of joy

I know it's not me, it's my master and I am

at his feet

I've climbed the high mountains

and I've swam the deep blue sea

I'm in the grace of mercy
and I almost can't believe that this is
happening to me
Count your blessings every little soul
Count your blessings
because God has contributed unto you gold
This may not seem real to you or to me
but the Holy Spirit above and beneath
has surely played his role
and lead us to total victory
I shall challenge you my children
and supply all of your needs
It need not make sense to you, for I
Understand in Jesus name Amen

# “My Vision”

## "My Vision"
### (Statement of Opinion)

Do you know how I vision life now? I see this wall not very long but tall. It sits in the middle of the earth, people on both sides. On my left there is the world in which we view in the natural and on my right there is the supernatural where we view in the spirit. When we were created, we were all put on the left side of the wall (where there is darkness) to see who would make it over to the right (where there is light). We were given a bag of resources that included weapons such as the bible, prayer, the choice to serve God, stand in his protection (under his covering that is) and receive the anointing of the Holy Spirit, to guide us in our endeavors.

Here we go climbing the wall of hope and out of darkness comes a force trying to restrain us from getting over to the other side, so we reach down in our bag of resources and pull out a weapon (prayer) oh it's on now; we think we can do this but are not really sure. In the meantime, another force comes against us even stronger than the one before, to keep us down. Now we are really worried, so we pull out yet another weapon (the bible) only this time we don't

use it enough, so it serves half its purpose and we are not as strong as we could and should be. That's when the forces get even stronger. They come at us full force lurking, waiting to see how many of us it can devour. We can't withstand the tension of this force on our own but as we make the choice to serve God and stand in his protection, he blesses us. He guides us, through the anointing of the Holy Spirit, to help us through what seems to be the hardest and trying times of our lives. In the end
we all know "who" really wins.

Now that's blessed! Speak the word upon your life, know where you are going and it will open doors. I am a winner and so are you. Choose to be blessed beyond the norm today.

**READ YOUR WORD! IT GIVES YOU FAITH!**

"Consequently, faith comes from hearing the message, and the message is heard through the word of Christ." **Romans 10:17 NIV Study Bible**

## “Crawl behind the window of faith”

Behind every story there is a lesson to learn, Some you may have heard and some you may have discerned. On my journey towards Galilee, Jesus came and set me free. He opened my eyes by a wing and a prayer. I stand on to tell others what great gifts we do have. I opened my eyes and the blue days are gone. I’ve never felt a fire so deep down within and as I take my place on this journey I can’t do anything but win. My source says to tell you, you have been set free and on your trip to Galilee, you must believe in thee. Waste no more time; get back into the boat. Let your gifts take you to places you have never seen before. Remember to stay focused and God will deliver your dreams right to your front door.

**“Jesus you are the love of my life”**

## “Jesus you are the love of my life”
### (My Gratitude)

Man, where should I start I thought; as I sat down to write this letter. “Jesus is the love of my life” is the revelation I received one Saturday morning October 9, 2004 to be exact. I’ll never forget this day. I was lying on my sofa and for two nights prior I had awakened out of my sleep by the unction of the Holy Spirit. I began to talk to my God as my heart felt led to do. I didn’t know why he kept awakening me out of my sleep, but I knew that it was for a good reason. You know that saying I was looking for love in all the wrong places? Well, it’s totally true.

You see, all of my life I just wanted for someone special to love me unconditionally. I also wanted someone I could love. As I was lying on the sofa I started to get emotional with God. The first thing I remembered was the scripture I can do all things through Christ Jesus who strengthens me (Philippians 4:13). It really touched my heart. I was worried about studying for my Real estate and cosmetology state boards when I realized the meaning of that scripture.

I kept saying Lord it's not me it's you and I can do all things through you. Through you I can pass my exams and I meditated on that for a moment. Then all of a sudden my heart started to tingle and I felt that intense need again to be loved by someone special. I wanted to get closer to God. I began to realize that it was not man that I needed this love from; especially the man that I thought would be my husband and whom I had been praying for. At that point I didn't want to feel needy anymore, so I literally cried out to God expressing my love for him and asking him to return his love unto me.

My heart was hurting and I asked him to fill the void so that I would never be in desperate need of the love of man again. It only took a second and it was done. The pain was gone and I knew that I could still love others without expecting them to return that love back unto me. I always knew that the love that I had inside of me was from God. It was the great gift that he had given me to give to others, but as the years went by and from rejection after rejection, at times I didn't want to love anymore. I couldn't understand how people could be so cruel, but we all know who the author is behind that.

Today is your day so receive the one true love of God that he wants so deeply to share with you. I'm telling you it soothes the soul, and for that I am grateful.

## How much does God love me?

More than words can ever say

More than darkness that turns into day

More than the cattle's on the hill

More than Jesus is real

More than my mind can consume

It takes all of me to be in love with you

That's how much God loves me

More than my breath that can be taken away

More than darkness that turns into day

More than wealth and riches that has

brought some to doom

More than a bride loves her groom

More than words can ever say, More than

his glory that has fulfilled this place

It is to my understanding that all my needs

are met I must trust in him for he has honored his word, For he has brought me out of a dark and lonely place, For he has brought me out and unto my wealthy place That's how much God loves me

**“Now I know why she couldn’t love me unconditionally”**

## “Now I know why she couldn’t love me unconditionally”

### Story #1

As a little girl, Priscilla was a loving child who cared about other people’s feelings. It didn’t matter to her who they were or what they were about. As she gave her love unconditionally, for so many years and trusted in those that she loved, one by one they slowly broke her heart. It started with her parents, who are supposed to love you for who you are, no matter what. Her father was an alcoholic and her mother favored her older sister Tammy, whom she had by another man. At times her parents would argue and fight so horribly, that it would only make Priscilla want to run away.

Priscilla loved her sister, but as time went on, she would get punished for things that her sister Tammy wouldn’t admit to doing. It made Priscilla feel depressed and lonely. She felt as if no one loved or cared for her at all. There was only one person that Priscilla could turn to besides God (her mother’s sister Aunt Bunny). Aunt Bunny would always try to make Priscilla feel special by letting her know how much she cared. Priscilla appreciated her love but she still felt alone.

It wasn't until she met her first love Ryan (who was four years older than Priscilla) that she would begin to feel secure in the love that the two of them would share. They were so excited and in love that they did everything together. They were inseparable. Priscilla knew in her heart that they were meant to be together. As the love between Priscilla and Ryan grew stronger, they became intimate with each other. For a while Priscilla began to shy away from her friends and especially her family.

It was because she was hiding a very big secret. At age 15, Priscilla became pregnant. She was afraid to tell anyone because she didn't want her parents to find out. She knew what their reaction would be. For seven months Priscilla hid her pregnancy. She only felt the need to tell Ryan, as she knew he would be happy. Priscilla would wear big clothing so that no one would notice how big her stomach was getting. She didn't go to the doctor for her prenatal care until she was about eight months into the pregnancy.

It wasn't until then, that she thought about telling her parents. She knew that they would find out sooner or later and she wanted the news to come from her. Ryan wanted to do the right thing and marry Priscilla. He wanted the two of them to give the news about the baby and the marriage to Priscilla's parents together, but Priscilla thought that it might be best to tell them on her own. One day as Priscilla was waiting for her parents to get home from work, she began to pray and ask God to help her with breaking the news to her parents.

Just as she finished praying, her mother walked through the door. Priscilla was afraid, so she decided to wait and tell her parents together when her father came home. Shortly thereafter her father came staggering through the door. He smelled of liquor. It was apparent that he had been drinking. Priscilla felt that this was her only opportunity to tell them or she wouldn't be able to do it at all. As she set her parents down to tell them the news her mother began to cry. Her father was outraged and began yelling at her.

He told her that if she decided to have the baby, she would have to move out. Priscilla was hurt and distraught but she left her home to marry Ryan and give birth to their child. One month later Priscilla gave birth to a beautiful baby girl and named her Traci. At first things were going well, but baby Traci suffered with asthma. Ryan had previously joined the U.S. Navy and was out at sea a lot. It was a warm summer day. Priscilla and her in-laws had to rush Traci to the hospital on post in Fort Lee, Virginia, where they found out that she had a case of meningitis.

The doctors weren't expecting baby Traci to make it through the night. The family contacted Ryan's commanding officer, so that he could come home to be by Traci and Priscilla's side. As they waited for him to arrive, Traci went into a coma. The doctors told Priscilla that she wouldn't come out and if by some miracle she did, she would only be a vegetable. She would not be able to function on her own. Priscilla kept her faith in God to whom she prayed to, to save her baby girl. As she ended the prayer, she looked up and to her surprise Traci lifted her foot in the air for her mother to kiss it (this was something that Priscilla did to show her love for Traci at times).

Priscilla began to jump for joy and she thanked God over and over. She shouted to the doctors My baby is alive! My baby is alive! The doctors knew that it was just that, a miracle. It wasn't long before Traci would be ready to go home from the hospital. Ryan was still on leave, but when it was time for him to return to sea, he didn't want to leave Traci's side. He refused to go back and got out of the service on a dishonorable discharge. He really didn't know what to do with his life after that, other than to be the best father that he could be to Traci.

He began to hangout and party with his friends a lot, which made Priscilla feel alone once again. She expressed to Ryan how she didn't like him hanging out all the time doing nothing. Of course he didn't want to hear that, so whenever Priscilla would talk to him about it, they would argue and it would lead up to a fight. They seemed to be growing apart. It got to the point where, every time Ryan would play with baby Traci, Priscilla would get jealous and says to Ryan; you love her more than you love me.

They continued to live together and ended up having another child this time a boy (Ryan Jr.). The relationship got worse and after the many fights that they had (where Ryan would sometimes beat Priscilla until she bleed) they separated. Ryan insisted that Priscilla would encourage the fights because she was so jealous of even her own children. Eventually they divorced and Priscilla's heart was broken once again. She set out to raise her two children all on her own. Priscilla got a job at a hospital for the handicapped and disturbed.

She was making good money, but she had to work long hours. It took a lot of time away from her children. The short time that Priscilla had to spend with her children meant a lot to them all. When Ryan Sr. and Priscilla's mother found out the long hours that she had to work, they immediately tried to use it against her to have her children taken away from her. They took her to court and told the judge that she was unfit to raise her children. Ryan was trying to get custody of Traci and Ryan Jr.

This would mean that Priscilla would be left alone and broken hearted once again. Priscilla loved her children too much for them to be taken away, so she quit her job and decided to go back to school part-time to get her nursing license. She eventually started dating again and when Ryan Sr. and her mother found out they set out to destroy her happiness. Priscilla could never keep a man. She had one broken relationship after the other. It became so stressful for her at times. She would get angry when things did not go right in her relationships and take it out on her children.

She would punish them for stupid things, because she was mad. Traci at age seven had taken enough and decided that she wanted to live with her father. She didn't want to leave Ryan Jr. because he was the youngest, but he decided to stay. Priscilla was angry about Traci's decision but she decided to let her go anyway. One more person that Priscilla cared about had walked out of her life. It was the beginning of life long disappointments for Priscilla. She had become withdrawn. She married three more times and none of her marriages lasted.

She had a relationship with another man that she did not marry and got pregnant with her third child Tony. During the third marriage, she was married to a guy named Bruce who was in the U.S. Army. He loved Priscilla so much and would do anything he could to make sure that his family was taken care of. He tried to give Priscilla and her two boys the world. At times things were extremely tight but they managed to make it through. They were stationed over in Germany for three years and to Priscilla, things were beginning to look better for her.

Traci was still living with her father, who later remarried himself to a woman named Patrice. Patrice and Traci did not get along. Patrice was jealous of the love that Ryan Sr. had for his daughter. For some reason neither, Patrice or Priscilla could understand that Traci was daddy's little (and only) girl. Patrice also thought that Ryan loved Traci more than her. It made things difficult and Patrice would be mean to Traci to get even. Sometimes Traci and Patrice both tried hard to get along to please Ryan Sr. but they just couldn't see eye to eye.

Traci despised her father's wife and rebelled against her. When Traci was fourteen, her father got into some trouble and went to jail for two years. Traci was left in the care of Patrice and her family. She really had it rough then. Patrice looked at it as her opportunity to get back at Traci for being the light in her father's life. She would be mean to Traci and even tried to fight her. She tried to hit Traci with a belt buckle and as Traci reached up her hand to block the hit, the buckle hit her on the finger and left a blood clot.

Traci vowed that day that she would not return home from school. After school let out she walked to her aunt's house nearby and told her what happened. Traci insisted on staying with her aunt until Priscilla could come back to the United States to get her. At age fifteen, Traci moved back in with her mother. They were stationed in Fort Stewart, Georgia for three years. Traci had a cousin named Steve who she was very close to. He was like a brother to her. Steve and Traci didn't want to separate so Steve moved to Georgia with Traci and her family. The two of them always looked out for each other.

Steve had two sisters of his own, but they weren't as close as Traci and Steve was. They could tell each other anything and wouldn't have to worry about it getting out. Everything was going fine and suddenly out of nowhere things got tight and Bruce began to change. He became verbally abusive to Priscilla and sometimes physically abusive. The children all started to hate him for that and they began to rebel. Things got worse. It was the beginning of the end of another relationship for Priscilla. Bruce started cheating and it wasn't until Priscilla mistakenly found out that he admitted to it.

They decided to go their separate ways. Priscilla was reluctant to start over again, but she did what she had to do. She decided to move back to her hometown in Petersburg, Virginia. Her life began to go down hill more every day. She only had a few clothes and $100 when she left Bruce. She moved in temporarily with her sister Tammy who lived with her two daughters and their (Priscilla and Tammy's) mother. The house was crowded and Priscilla had no other choice but to find a job and a place of her own for her and her children to live.

During this time Ryan Sr. had been out of jail for one year and was back living with his wife Patrice. Traci moved in with the two of them to release some of the stress off of Priscilla. Priscilla eventually found a job working in a store and moved into a two-bedroom apartment over the store. It was only enough room for her and the boys. Traci visited them often. Tony and Ryan Jr. was growing up and starting to discover themselves. They began to get in trouble and didn't care if it would hurt Priscilla.

They just thought they were having fun. Tony wasn't as bad as Ryan Jr. he did a few sneaky things, but nothing compared to what Ryan Jr. was getting into. He just didn't care. He was fighting, stealing, lying, hanging out with the wrong crowd and staying out all night. Priscilla was devastated because even though she had been through so much in her life and with her children, she tried her best and taught them right from wrong. It was their choice to make the right decisions in life.

She did all she could do. For many years to come Ryan Jr. would be in and out of detention centers. At age 21 he was convicted of another devastating crime. Tony began to follow in his footsteps, got in trouble and ended up in jail himself. It wasn't until Tony had to serve his time in jail that he realized that he didn't want to follow in his brother's footsteps after all. Priscilla had such a hard life and she trusted in other people so much. All they did was hurt her. It made her a cold hearted and bitter woman.

Her daughter Traci got married and had children of her own. Traci always felt like she could depend on her mother whenever she needed her. She thought she could tell her anything. Traci would confide in her mother. Priscilla would act sympathetic and even give her advice. You could see the strife in Priscilla's eyes. Traci couldn't understand why her mother would react to her this way. Traci knew that her mother wasn't the same loving person anymore. They both got mad at each other at times, but Traci still believed in her mother.

She trusted Priscilla and got hurt over and over again. Traci began to have bad feelings of her own about her mother. She prayed to God to help her deal with Priscilla without feeling anger or hatred. Traci loved her mother and even felt sorry for her. She often wondered how a mother could be that way to her own child. The two of them weren't close for a long time. As Traci reached her late twenties, she gave her life over to the Lord and learned how to forgive others no matter what they have done.

Priscilla also had been going to church, but she couldn't completely get rid of the anger that she had been carrying around for so many years. It was sad for Traci to hear her mother say that she trusted and believed in God but not enough to forgive. They would talk all the time. It wasn't until a conversation that they had over the phone, that Traci would finally realize why her mother couldn't love her unconditionally. Her mother had built a wall around her heart to protect herself and if it meant that others would get hurt in the process, well, it really didn't matter to Priscilla anymore.

Traci still loves her mother and prays for her often. She believes that one day her mother will be able to love again without fear of getting hurt. It is important to open your heart to forgiveness or it will keep you in bondage. Are you ready to forgive?

**“God help me to understand, rebuild and keep my self-esteem”**

## “God help me to understand, rebuild and keep my self-esteem”

**(One woman’s experience with the lost of her self-esteem)**

What is self-esteem?

Webster’s Dictionary and Roget’s Thesaurus describes it as the esteem or good opinion of oneself.

Webster’s II New Riverside University Dictionary’s definition: Satisfaction with oneself.

The American Heritage Dictionary’s Definition: Pride in oneself.

Then let’s look at self-confident:

Webster’s New World Children Dictionary’s Definition: Sure of oneself; Confident of one’s own ability.

When you look at these definitions you can see that self-esteem is how you actually feel about who you are and being self-confident is being sure of yourself. Let me start out by saying it takes two to tangle, two to give and two to receive. Relationships are a two way street. You should always give 100/100% not 50/50%. This is my opinion, and I say this because 100% is your best. 50% is only half your best. It takes 100% to be whole and we all need to be whole, so that, when we come together with our God ordained significant other (spouse) the relationship will be double the blessings.

## Introduction

Every since I was a little girl I've had big dreams. I wanted to do so many things. I was interested in becoming a model, actress, professional singer, director/producer, hair stylist, real-estate salesperson and a loving wife and mother. Somehow I felt empowered and enthused that I could accomplish all these goals at some point in my life. After graduating high school I began to take courses in some of my fields of interest. I took one class after the other but never was able to complete any of my goals. As the years passed and being that I got married at such a young age, I saw my dreams as being so far off, but I always held on to the hope of someday making it real.

## "Running to the altar to satisfy my flesh"

Story #2

I was a young girl (seventeen to be exact) just graduating high school, feeling good about myself for being the first in my family to graduate. I had my heart and mind set on being the best that I could be, setting goals and making every effort in my heart to accomplish them. Then it happened! I fell in love with Johnny. So much so that I didn't care what I was getting myself into. I thought that I could live with whatever was going to happen in my life as long as Johnny and I were together. Nothing else mattered.

I believed that we could get through anything. Being constantly reminded by others that having an intimate relationship with a man without marriage was definitely a sin; I was even more eager to get married because I didn't want to disappoint anyone, mainly God. I felt like I was betraying him. So low and behold I put my foot down and refused to carry on the relationship until we were married. I had already given birth to our first son and thought why not tie the knot. By age twenty-one we did it. We got married. Everything seemed ok at first.

I was finally getting what my heart desired (so I thought) a family of my own, whom I could love and would love me back. I didn't stop to think. We were already having hard times and financial difficulties. All I knew was that whatever happened as long as Johnny and I stuck together, we could make it; and we did, barely. We were struggling from paycheck to paycheck, moving from house to house, driving car after car. After we had been in jeopardy of repossession, we decided to turn the cars in. It took a toll on the entire family because by the fourth year of our marriage, Johnny and I had two more children.

I couldn't work at times having small children. I didn't have anyone dependable to baby-sit. I'd work for a short period of time and then have to stop to be home with the children while Johnny worked. He was a good man and was all about taking care of his family. After a while it was even more stressful for him, being that he already had an alcohol and occasional drug habit. Things got worse. I was alone a lot and would get depressed because I didn't see Johnny much and felt as if he was missing out on the most important parts of our lives. At times I felt as though we were merely roommates. My self-esteem was slowly fading away.

I didn't realize it at the time because all I could think about was being strong for my family at whatever cost. I cried out to God on a regular basis. I would ask God why was this happening to me and when was he going to make the changes in my husband that I had been praying for. As the years passed by, I would pray even more for my husband and our marriage; but the more I prayed the further apart we grew. I had lost my identity. I'd forgotten about the goals that I set and all I knew was that I had to make the marriage work.

Johnny himself began to lose his identity, but instead of pressing into God as I had done, he decided that he would take matters into his own hands. His heart was unwilling and our lives started going in different directions. We had been sharing a house with some of my relatives when we decided that we would be better off moving to Johnny's hometown in Hopewell, Virginia and finding a small apartment of our own. Johnny was more excited about the move then I was. Prior to us moving, I was asleep in bed one morning, when I began to have a dream about Johnny leaving me.

It terrified me. I woke up out of the dream with my heart hurting so badly; I thought it was the devil messing with me so I started rebuking the dream. That following week I had the same dream only this time I could see Johnny walking away towards a car. I cried out to him; Johnny please don't leave me, no don't go! I couldn't get to Johnny because there were people holding me back telling me to let him go. Johnny turned and looked at me and then with his head hanging down looking sad he began to walk away. It was as if he didn't want to hurt me but he had to go.

It was something he had to do. Again I woke up out of my dream with an aching heart. As I began to pray about the dream Johnny walked in the room and asked me what was wrong. I explained; Johnny, I just had this awful dream. I dreamed that you were leaving me. Johnny looked at me in a strange way but didn't utter a word. He slowly walked out of the room. I didn't think about it anymore but Johnny knew that I wasn't just having a bad dream. It was God preparing me for what was about to happen.

Johnny had been having an affair for two months. He was only interested in moving back to his hometown to be closer to his lover. He had thoughts about leaving me but was also having doubts. Two months later we moved back to Hopewell and Johnny began to stay out late. One weekend he didn't come home at all. I was upset but all I could do was pray. I didn't know why Johnny would stay away for so long. I didn't want to stress about it because I was use to him staying out all night on occasion. Finally that Sunday evening Johnny came home.

I felt in my heart that something wasn't right because Johnny was very distant. I tried talking to him but he wouldn't respond. I thought that I had done something wrong to make Johnny stay out all weekend. As it began to get late, I decided that I would turn in for the night and asked Johnny if he was going to bed as well. Johnny didn't even look at me, he just said nope in a cold and aggressive voice. I knew that what I felt in my heart was true. I asked Johnny why? Do you have someone else? He responded yep! I asked him where he had been over the weekend.

Where do you think Johnny said; I was with my lover. I was shocked. As my heart shattered to pieces, I ran to my room. I really didn't know how to respond, because I would have never thought in a million years that this would be happening to me. I took my marriage vows seriously. I was very angry, hurt and afraid. I hung my head down and with my face in the palms of my hands I began to cry Lord, what is happening to me? What did I do wrong? How can I make it better? Is my marriage over? Oh Lord; I am so afraid to be alone. Suddenly there was a knock at the door. It was some of Johnny's relatives.

He began to talk with them as though nothing had happened. I came out of the room for fear of being embarrassed. I wiped my eyes and acted as if nothing was wrong. In my mind I was praying to God, hoping that they would hurry up and leave so that I could continue grieving; after all it had felt like I had just lost my best friend. After our company left, I asked Johnny if he was moving out and he said yes, again speaking in an aggressive tone. I couldn't understand why he was showing so much anger towards me, when I hadn't done anything to hurt him. He was so uncaring.

It was as if he was being aggressive so that I would get upset and argue back to lift the burden of guilt off of him for what he had done. I refused to react in such a manner. All I could think about was what am I going to do now? All the years and all the drama I went through, but I still hung in there with Johnny as I had vowed to do. I thought that God would make it right. Well, he did; it just wasn't the way I had expected. Every time I would pray to God about helping my husband with his problems before he got old; God would minister things to me about my husband that didn't fit his character.

I thought that maybe God was going to make him this wonderful man that my heart desired, the man whom he called him to be but little did I know. I always prayed my husband, my husband and that's what God was doing; preparing my husband whom he had ordained, not the one I had chosen to marry on my own. It had taken me some time to realize what God was doing; so I held on to the hope of putting my marriage back together. I continued to pray to God and confess God's promises for my marriage.

I was holding on to this hope for dear life. I refused to give in to the temptation of getting back at Johnny for the affair. I decided instead to keep my hands clean and let the Lord fight my battle. After all it was him who said that he would make my enemies a footstool at my feet (Psalm 110:1). I had been separated from Johnny for five months. To me this was a nightmare. I was in constant pain, always blaming myself for the separation. I grieved daily as if I had lost the most important thing in my life. I loved Johnny so much.

I couldn't believe that he had turned his back on the children and I. Johnny didn't come around much to visit and I felt bad because he had been in our lives from the children's birth up until our oldest son was eleven years old. I didn't know where to begin the healing process for my children and myself. I pressed into God day in and day out; always trying to keep busy to take my mind off of things, but feeling so hurt and lonely. I stayed away from everyone, especially my family. I didn't want to hear anything negative that anyone had to say.

I was into the church when all of this had taken place, so I began to seek God more and fellowshipped constantly with my Christian brothers and sisters. I felt that I needed to be in a positive environment with positive people; where I could freely express myself without fear. Every day and night I would cover my children (and husband) with the word of God and we started having family prayer in a circle. Everyone would express to God how he or she was feeling about what had taken place in our lives.

With the support of God and my Christian family, I began a slow process of healing. I had to take it one day, one step at a time. Most times it was a battle (a living hell) to keep my sanity. Every time I pressed into God, the attacks came, full force from every direction. Through it all, I remembered with the unctioning of the Holy Spirit, not to give up. In the end God prevailed and the breakthroughs and deliverances began to come. It was time to go to the next level. How wonderful and energized I felt only to be faced with yet another devil.

I was eager for God to bring out the things that he had placed in me no matter what it cost. The enemy would sometimes attack my mind and heart with so much pain. I had gotten extremely tired and all I could say was; if I could only go to sleep for just a little while, when I wake up it will all be over. The pain would be gone. Not so! I would have gone to sleep and never waken up. I cried out to God; Lord, please help me. I can't take this pain anymore. Gradually as God began to heal my wounds and show me things that I had in me that was not of him, I would confess these things to him and God would deliver me.

I was always going through some test, having breakthroughs and getting delivered. At one time I felt as if I was on an emotional rollercoaster; not being able to get off until the ride finished. As I grew closer to God he began to show me how beautiful I was inside. He led me to a scripture that identified the fruit of the spirit. But the fruit of the spirit is love, joy, peace, patience, kindness, goodness, faithfulness, gentleness and self control (NIV study bible- Galatians 5:22-23). God encouraged me to be honest with myself and search my heart to see if I possessed these qualities.

I began to take a deeper look within myself and as challenges came my way I would compare how I handled the situations in my own heart against the fruit of the spirit. It was then that I began to see where I needed to put forth an effort (by confessing and being obedient) so that God could make the necessary adjustments in my heart. As God began to shed off the old and put on the new, I could see myself in a different light. I loved music and singing, so I decided to join the praise team at my church. Being in such an important leadership position took a lot of consistent praying.

For me it was my first time singing with anyone and I didn't know what to expect. It helped me to grow spiritually because I knew that I couldn't begin to minister to the people without the help of the Holy Spirit. I meditated on God and allowed his spirit to flow through me to touch others. Singing also made me happy. If it wasn't for God, the church and me singing on the praise team, I would have never made it through the most painful times that I had to endure when my marriage fell apart. I tried daily to focus on God and his will for my life.

I gradually began to regain my self-esteem and self-confidence. I still thought about Johnny at times and at one point thought that I had truly forgiven him. Until one day God showed me that I was still holding on to that anger. I denied it at first, but as the attacks on my mind increased, I knew that I had to recognize and get rid of the anger. I didn't show any anger or hatred towards Johnny when everything happened so, I would always relate back to that moment and the pain would get worse. I then admitted to God what was inside of my heart and he freed me from that anger. I could then go on with my life.

I kept having bad dreams, one behind the other, week after week, about Johnny and I getting back together. Things hadn't changed. In fact, they had gotten worse. I woke up out of my dream one day with my heart hurting and I said Lord, I can't go through that. So I prayed in the spirit and in the midst of my prayer God said let go of your past. I knew exactly what he was talking about but I kept telling myself that I must have misunderstood and so I put it off for a while until he told me again to let it go.

Johnny came to visit me to tell me that he was coming back home (not long after the dreams) I gave him a second chance and it only lasted two weeks. The first week was good; the second week Johnny started cheating with his lover again. This time I put him out and I refused to take him back. I remembered the dreams and what God had told me. I knew then what I had to do, so I immediately filed for a divorce. It was like a pound of weights lifted off of my shoulders. Johnny didn't take too kindly to my decision, in fact, he didn't even know if he really wanted a divorce. I was friends with Johnny even after all that we had been through.

I knew that one day he would reap the harvest for the seed he had sown. At times I would be led to pray for Johnny and his lover (now that's God). To my surprise marriage was not as easy as I thought. Marriage is special, very serious and should be sought and ordained by God. You take on responsibilities that should be well planned and organized. Marriage should be set on a solid foundation based on the word of God to be successful in the growing process.

It doesn't mean that you won't have troubles, but seeking God for guidance will preserve strength, sound mind, judgment, discernment and direction in building a healthy relationship and environment, especially when making the decision to have children. Never give up hope. Hold on to faith and continue to press towards the mark to win the prize that God has called you heaven forward. Hold on until God shows you something different.

**“Is he the one?”**

## "Is he the one?"
### Story #3

As I searched my heart to find out what I wanted out of life; what I wanted in a man (the man) the one that I had been praying to God to bring into my life, it suddenly hit me. How was I ready to deal with the real thing (brought and ordained by God) if I hadn't gotten myself in order? Man that seemed impossible to do. I wanted everything that my heart desired, but I didn't want to let go of some of the little things, which really seemed big to me at the time. I guess you could say I wanted to have my cake and eat it too.

It only brought more frustration, stress and confusion. I had been hurt so much throughout life and all I wanted was to settle down with my God, a husband and my children. Over the years, five to be exact, I had been dealing with this guy on a friendship basis. We could talk about anything and it felt good to be able to express ourselves to one another, vent or whatever the case would be. We really did care a lot about each other. Everything was cool until we started having sex. It was our way of releasing stress from things or people we had endured during the week.

It wasn't a consistent thing, it was occasional. I guess that's what made it seem all right. It only happened when it was convenient for both of us, which was cool or so I thought. After time had passed and feelings started to get in the way, I had to take a second look at myself and ask "Is this what I want for the rest of my life"? It suddenly made me sick to know that I had lowered myself for so long, only because I was lonely and hurt. It made me feel good at the time so in some ways I didn't even care. Eventually I wanted more but not with him.

He was really just a good friend, not even my type. I still cared about him for who he was and because of the love of God in me. At one point, it was hard for me to say no. It was because I had been saying yes for so long. I truly had to force myself to ignore his phone calls and then let my cell phone go because I knew that if my phone rang (and it was him) I was going to be in trouble, or I would call him myself. I had to find some way to break the cycle. After a while the thoughts of having sex with him went away. I was relieved. I could then continue my healing process with no interruptions and prepare for my future.

The year 2006 was really ruff for me. My oldest son got himself into some trouble. For me it was hard and painful, having to go back and forth two times a week from one detention center to another. I had two other children to take care of along with a four-bedroom house and no job. I moved in with my children's cousin to try and get on my feet, but ended up in a motel. I was there for five months. This is where I met Brandon. He was visiting his sister at the time. We immediately took interest in each other, but I decided to hold back and stay focused. I didn't want to end up in another wrong relationship.

Within an instant, almost, we became a couple. Things were great and I knew in my heart that I loved him no matter what issues we had. I went through so much with him over the summer. I was serious about my calling so I continued to press into God. I asked Lord, is he the one? I could honestly see the love there but in a sense it scared me. I had gone through more with him than I had in any other relationship I've ever had. I would pray to God and say Lord this doesn't look like the kind of man I would have expected you to connect me with. It really bothered me, so I continued to pray.

I wanted the Lord to give me a sign or something to let me know if I was truly walking in his will. Three days later I was at work (at a beauty salon) when a woman that was a customer of one of the other stylists, came to get her hair done. Her regular stylist wasn't there so she asked me if I could do it. I saw the lady on one other occasion a few days before when she was in the shop visiting, (Brandon was escorting me through the door). We were joking around with the barber, laughing and having fun as we always did. In the back of my mind I was still thinking about the question I asked God, was he the one? As she sat in my chair she looked at me and began to minister to me.

She said, "You know the other day when I came in here, God gave me a word to give to you, but I wouldn't say anything. I wanted to be sure that it was him. He has been whipping my spirit ever since. I knew that I had no other choice but to tell you. The guy that brought you in here the other day, is that your friend she said? I replied yes. She then turned around and looked me in my eyes and said that God told her to tell me that he is the one. I started tripping at first. I wondered how she knew. I didn't know this lady at all. I could only believe that God does answer prayers. He sometimes sends word through people I thought. It had to be true. I didn't know what to do.

I smiled. She also said that I was going to go through some things with him but he is the one and to remember that the battle is not mine it's the Lords. I looked at her and said, but he has issues, and who doesn't she replied, "It's the heart that God looks at". I knew then that I wasn't in the situation on my own and that God had his hand on my relationship with this man. That's when I began to trust God even more. Who knows what obstacles we may have to endure, but with the love that we share and by the grace and mercy of God, everything will be alright. Stand firm and stay focused until God says yes.

# “A prayer to my Lord”

Lord you gave me this man to call my own We vowed to be together and not leave each other alone. To stick with one another through thick and thin, understanding and forgiving when one has sinned. I come to you in prayer Lord to pray for his soul. Please help him with his problems before he gets old. Make him a strong man in everything he does and when he is weak may he bow down to you.

**“Life is like a jigsaw puzzle”**

## "Life is like a jigsaw puzzle"

(Statement of Opinion)

Life is like a jigsaw puzzle. You know how you start out with all these loose pieces, trying to figure out where each one goes; sometimes putting pieces in the wrong places and getting frustrated because for the life of you, you can't seem to find the perfect match? Well, that's when God wants us to trust him. He takes us by the hand and slowly leads us (as long as we are willing) to that piece of the puzzle, then guides us to its perfect match. Wow! That's awesome.

You see, sometimes when we are allowing God to lead us by the spirit, he may give us bits and pieces to our life's puzzle and sometimes the human flesh part of us wants to try and figure things out before he can finish with us. No, no, no,no,no wrong answer. That's when we are to trust him, obey his word and follow his lead. There is no way in the world we can do anything in life, especially take the lead in the kingdom of God, stand on the battlefield, front and center, rooted and grounded; where God needs us to be without his help.

He leads us through all temptation, delivers us from all evil and we must not go our separate ways. We know we care about ourselves, we know we care about each other, but how do we know, how much we care about God? We are supposed to walk by faith and not by sight, yet sometimes we have a habit of looking back. We must understand that the tests of time are here and we are going to be tried in every way, shape and form. We must know that our only help comes from the Lord.

In addition to the things of God in our lives, we must discern the spirits of our youth. We must take pride in sharing the gifts of God with our children. We must operate in the spirit of the Lord always and we must not fail to give glory to his name. Abundance is in our household. We never seek to find things that we already have. We backslide, we pray, we act distant, we play, but the joke is on us if we think we are fooling anyone. God sees all. We taint the life of others by pretending we know it all.

Today I say, Lord, I trust you on this journey. You have absolute, complete and total control in the situations in my life. I am bound to you forever. I let loose the things of the flesh that would hurt our fellowship as well as our spiritual growth together. I take pride in the things of God in my life and I exalt you in the highest way, “Almighty”. I believe in you for everything that’s inside of me. I am conscious of my walk with you. I am being led by the spirit right now and I take no credit for what I write.

My thoughts are not your thoughts you say; so Lord, take my hand and lead the way. I drink from the cup of the fountain of life. I spread my wings and fly as high as I can go. I hear the sleigh bells ringing in the midnight hour. My faith is being tested. I get up and pray. No one can see me; I am far, yet near. I speak the truth and I bring blessings to one’s ears. I wait a few days. I walk out the door and no ones home. I’m starving for more. I see spiritual growth in my youth. I was so tired all those days.

I woke up this morning and I forgot to pray. I stood still for a moment; the Lord watched over me. My eyes have been opened and now I'm about to receive. I expect that it won't take very long but all I can think about is what's going through my head. To be free of depression; my soul is almost dead. I wake up in the middle of the night. I hold back no tears. I walk before the Lord. He brings back the most successful years. I speak out in his presence. I say things I don't mean. I am grieved by the spirit of satan; I continue to break out in tears.

I'm about to leave his presence now to go back home. I can't stay away any longer; I must go where Jesus goes. I am free to express myself in the most positive way. I place my hand in Jesus' hand and let him lead the way. I'm not perfect now, nor will I ever be, but the Jesus in me says I'm totally free. I can't seem to get back into the things I use to do. I can't believe this is me. My father says, yes; this is you. My heart is aching now that I am filled with the cup of love. I burst into tears. I open my eyes and I see the stars.

I make known the things of God, the things from afar. After the breastplate of righteousness, I have placed on my wings. I'm about to fly the highest mountains where they all can see me. Jesus loves me this I know. I never have to stay awake at night wondering why I've failed in life. I've succeeded in accomplishing my dream and we all know what that means. Yes, I am a success in Jesus name. I am what the word says I am and I no longer have to be ashamed. I strive to follow the will of God.

I make note of how he has brought me from afar, but still in my testing times I may sometimes wither. May he never let me fail for I am his own creation? Darkness had arisen in my life, but now the light shines more than ever before. I opened my eyes last night and I walked through that door. I hid behind the window of praise. I spelled out the things of God in my life. I've made mistakes. I've corrected them by his grace. The world has a lot to offer me; so I thought. Wow! Was I wrong, that's why Jesus' life had to be brought?

I can't thank him enough for all that he has done. Now I don't have to make ends meet, for my battle is already won. Next year I see myself going further in the eyes of the Lord. I take out the trash and let no one know where I'm going anymore. I'm frantic right now but I'm still holding on. Each day I open my eyes I shall be amazed. I see spirit lead people walking from every way. I'm about to sing a new song to my father and I am absolutely blessed. I challenge you today to stand and take the test.

Note; how Jesus led me in the spirit to write in his presence as though it was happening to me all over again. He knows what he is doing when he tells us to do something. I bring back the things of God (from the light) to my life and to yours. Where I know he awaits through opened, not closed doors. Eager to please him, I must say. Jesus you are so awesome and very special to me in every way. Thank you! I know it may seem as if you'll never hear Jesus but he's calling you from afar to bring you near.

The distance in between is where we believe we stand alone, but I say unto you today; please continue to hold on. The distance may seem long to you, very much so, but wait until he finishes; you will be glad you did. You shall be a blessing and you must take the lead. Get ready to receive, don't let your faith walk out that door. Build up your spirit man with the word. Take my word for what it's worth; it's all about Jesus the creator of all the earth. Distance yourself no longer from the perpetual kingdom of God.

Get in his face and get ready to laugh out loud. Whisper in his ear if you must, but stay close by, don't try to do this on your own for your carnal mind must surely die. It will overcome and subdue you; bringing all the darkness that it can surely breeze in. You see, you want the flesh to die; not the Holy Spirit that is within you. So stay alert and don't be afraid. Last but not least don't forget to pray. On the day that you read the end of this book, think of it as the beginning of you taking the challenge to become the new you.

Make every effort to take steps towards God by putting him first and listening to what he tells you. It won't be an easy ride or a smooth one; but at the finish line you shall take home the prize.

(NIV) Habakkuk 2:3- for the vision is yet for an appointed time, but at the end it shall speak and not lie; though it tarry, wait for it, because it will surely come, it will not tarry.

Jesus I thank you for birthing my testimony, through your eyes. Through your word, grace and mercy I shall continue to travel on as you continue to do a work in me until the day of Christ.

For God so loved the world that he gave his only begotten, son, that whosoever believeth in him shall not perish, but have everlasting life (John 3:16).

## “My greatest inspiration”

My greatest inspiration is the love of my life. My father in heaven I give him praise and delight. I don’t have to stand-alone and through him I am strong. He gives me hope when nothing or no one else comes through. My greatest inspiration my God, I love you. He is the highest power stronger than us all. There to pick us up when we stumble and fall. You are my greatest inspiration and I am proud to say,
Father thank you for taking my hand
and helping me along the way.

# “Testimonies in times of trouble”

# “Testimonies in times of trouble”

## Testimony 1

Just when I found out that he was sick, not knowing what to expect because he had never been sick before, I felt so empty, worried and lonely. I cried out to Jesus to make things o.k. I asked him to deliver my husband from his sickness (diabetes) and to strengthen him. I was standing on faith no matter what anyone else said. He started to get better and I kept on praying. I hadn’t been faithful to God. I was not paying my tithes like I should have been and I was not attending services on a regular basis either.

I felt very guilty and unworthy to ask the Lord for anything, but I asked for forgiveness and kept praying. I refused to give up. I know I can be worthy if I keep standing while the Lord fights my battles. (It’s not my work that blesses me, only his grace and mercy). As I am sitting here writing this, my eyes are watery and all I can do is pray. I am weak at this point and I have asked the Lord for the strength to do his will.

## Testimony 2

The Lord has really blessed me. I had to quit my day job and look for a night job to fit my family's schedule. At the time I was in a bind because my husband had to get a new car or he wouldn't have a job. I was behind on my bills and I didn't know how I would pay them. I stood out on faith and asked the Holy Spirit for guidance. Two weeks later, I had a 1998 Dodge Stratus, a new job paying more money and my bills were caught up.

## Testimony 3

I had no money and a $330 car note to pay. I told my finance company that I would pay them on June 13, 1999. I had not one dime and didn't know how I was going to come up with the money by this date. As I was driving down the road one day, listening to my favorite song; Morning, glory, peace; by Juanita Bynum, I was overwhelmed all of a sudden and I couldn't stop praising God. Tears were running from my eyes and my mind was fixed on the Lord. I didn't know how I ended up at my destination.

All I know is that I was there and I was high in the Spirit. When I got home I was still praising God and didn't know why. I kept saying thank you Jesus, that's all I could say. At one point I said Lord I don't know why I am praising you so uncontrollably, but I thank you anyway. A few moments later I could hear my mailman putting mail in the box. I went out to check it and all I saw was junk mail. It made me mad at first, but as I realized that this was only the work of the devil "me getting mad about junk mail being in a mailbox".

I let it go and asked for forgiveness. When I removed the mail from the box, I saw an envelope. It was a check for $365. I shouted thank you Jesus. It had come two days before June 13th. By the time the car payment would go through the mail, the finance company would receive it on the day God planned.

## Testimony 4

Here I am stuck in a small town, where my life is going nowhere. I prayed and asked God for a change according to his will. He delivered me from that small town and moved me to a better one. Things are looking up for my family and I. We only have God to thank for that. I'm still learning and the teaching is so anointing. We can all stand a change for the good in one-way or another. Let the Holy Spirit be your guide to our Lord and savior, by the grace of God.

# “Heartwarming prayers”

## Prayer I.

Oh Lord, my Lord, my heart cries out for the souls that are lost. Please hear my cry, oh Lord. Use me! Through my lips speak tender words to their ears so that they may hear and know it's you. I pray for the word, strength, faith and the power of your anointing to touch them and dwell within their souls. I stand strong in the gap, where their faith has wavered. Like a magnet, use me, to draw them back to you. I see millions and millions fall at your feet. That's why Satan tried to kill me three times in my sleep.

As I woke up gasping for air and calling on your name, you freed me from that pound of weight that was suffocating me. Satan knew that such a day as this would come, when I would break through the barriers, with strength drawn from you. Now I know there is nothing that I cannot do. I've come too far and I'll never turn back. I'll grab on to those that you place in my path to lead them to that narrow gate, so that you can carry them through. I'll do this Lord with all my heart. I'll do this just for you.

I'm upset Lord and I'm on a warpath to tear down everything that I see Satan trying to build and has built around me. When I see him I will call him out. I draw my strength from you Lord, because I know that this is not going to be easy. With your love and protection I know I'll be alright.

In Jesus name, Amen.

## Prayer II.

Dear father,
Oh how I praise your Holy name. You have the power and you deserve the glory from us all. I love you, need you and want you in my life forever. Take me Lord and do as you please. At times, I feel your power in an instant as I pray. You are so mighty and merciful and I am forever grateful. Every time I think of you, I cry tears of joy. I've opened my heart and you've filled every void. When I am wrong, oh how you convict my soul. It doesn't feel good but I am here to stay. It may take some time but I want to do things your way.

In Jesus name, Amen.

# “Poems”

# “The cover over my eyes”

I have a cover over my eyes it is like a venetian blind, I can open and shut them through good and bad times. I am the only one that can control them because they’re mine, You see,  I have control of what my eyes unwind. I look for the positive and block out the negative but sometimes I have to open them halfway to see what both sides portrays. Things are not always what they seem to be but with the cover over my eyes I can be me.

## “Is green $ the cause of my pain?”

Would it be insane to say that a whole lot of green would make my day? When times are hard and there is nothing I can do, it really hurts and you know this is true. Will it make me a better person or will it corrupt my mind? Will I have any comfort in all the green $ that I shall find? Is green $ the cause of my pain?

## “The pain that he feels”

The pain that he feels is oh so strong
Thinking no one cares so he does things
Wrong. What can I do to make things better
I feel the pain that he feels so I will write
him a letter. In the meantime I can’t stop
crying. Does he really know in my heart I
am dying? I love my brother very much
I wish I could reach out to him and his heart
is what I would touch. Things are not the
same anymore. Hearts have been broken
and doors have been closed. I hope this is
not the end because as long as I live
my brother will always be my friend.

## “Up up to heaven”

Pick me up, put me down

Dress me in that long white gown

Put my wings on and let me flow to the

lost behind me I will help them grow

Up up to heaven, up up and away

Up up to heaven for that very special day

## “Wake up Joanne”

Wake up Joanne, this is not you

You’re sleeping on life and you’re always

Blue. Don’t let your troubles keep you

Down. Wake up Joanne and wipe off that

Frown. It’s a new day and there’s always a

way God said so and all you have to do is

pray. I remember the times when you would

laugh tripping off of others while looking

out for their behalf. Your life was so full of

joy just knowing that you had one girl and

two boys. Wake up Joanne, because there’s

much more waiting for you behind that

golden door.

## “Depression”

Depression is something that we all sometimes feel not knowing what to do, not knowing what is real. We stay to ourselves and that’s not right, put all that nonsense behind you and stand up and fight. Open your eyes because there are better days. Open your eyes and you will be amazed. If you are depressed, don’t stand-alone, look deep into your heart and find the Holy Spirit to lean on. Keep in mind that God loves you For you are his child and there is nothing he can’t do. May God bless you each and everyday, talk to him, because depression is not the way.

## "Why does she stay?"

Why does she stay, when he cheated and threw her a way? Time after time she let him come back, scared of what he might do so she set herself up for the trap. Never thinking of the consequences she always did what he wanted, now their lives are so messed up full of lies, suspicion and tormenting. Will things ever be the same? or will he continue to call the other woman's name? Why does she stay? It's beginning to sound like a broken record. Asking the same question, but never knowing what to say. Why does she stay? When he cheated and threw her a way.

## “My precious feelings”

Feelings are so precious

Even more than you know

My feelings are important

and I have to let them show

I can’t remember a time when I couldn’t feel

Whether it was love, anger or fear

My feelings are real

You take them for granted and that’s o.k. to

I just hope you wake up before someone

does it to you

I don’t mean to sound harsh or even cold

but my feelings are precious and you should

treat them like they’re gold

## “The reflections of my heart”

Look around, look around, oh what do you see? The reflections of my heart, how could this be? Is it because I put you before myself Or when we argue I apologize to keep peace and comfort in our lives? Even when the toughest times are near, I stand strong by your side and all is back in gear. In life we never know how much we will grow but in any event the reflections of my heart will always show. Look around, look around, oh what do you see? The reflections of my heart, “Yes this is me”.

## "Time is running out"

Time is running out or didn't you know? Throw away those pipes and stop snorting that blow. Out of your mind and can't even remember your name, don't you know that it's time to make a change? Put that cup down and stop sipping on that booze, over indulging yourself because you're afraid to lose. Keep your legs closed and stop letting everyone in blaming it on stress and saying, but he's my friend. Respect the person who made it possible for you to be here and stop having babies from New year to New year.

Commit to your children while they are Young so they won't do the things you have done. Time is running out or didn't you know? You better make up your mind, which way you will go.

## “Choices”

Choices are mine and choices are yours

Choices will open all kinds of doors

Choices are to be made carefully

Sometimes you don’t even think

Not realizing that choices can take you’re

life before you can blink

Some choices are great and some are not

So when you make a choice think and pray a

lot

# "Giving back"

Giving back not to be rewarded but from the heart is what it's all about. My community needs me they're slowly dying out. If the love I have is what they need to survive, then I will give to them all if it will save their lives. I look all around me and I see children dying, babies hungry and crying dope dealers and users, pregnant teens and spouse abusers. It makes me mad to see these things going on so I am going to pray for my community, that God will give them the strength to carry on. Giving back can be a very powerful tool. Giving back just might save you.

## "To my family"

You are all more than just blood to me

You are the light in my life

You are the joy that up lifts me

You make me smile and sometimes you

make me mad, I love all of you even when

you have been bad

I will always love you all no matter what

But I have to admit sometimes you're a pain

in my butt

# "A friend"

A friend, huh, what does that mean? At this point in time, I can honestly say that's me. Those who don't know me think I'm too sensitive. What about you are you as judgmental? Some of you have forgotten what it means to be a friend, can't wait until I turn my back so you can quickly shove a knife in. It seems easy that way because you're not obligated to trust. You're not sincere because your heart has been crushed. I guess you would say that it's my problem always thinking that we are suppose to love and be faithful to one another. You call yourself a friend, huh, that's a big joke. Your license has been suspended and your friendship is revoked.

I'm so glad that I'm not caught up in the rut with all the unhappy people in this world who don't know when to shut up. Whispering when another walks by and when they turn around you smile, while looking them in the eye. A friend, huh, what does that mean? At this point in time I can honestly say that's me.

## "That everlasting fear"

When I was a young girl, I had lots of
Dreams, wanting to do so many things, but
couldn't get pass that everlasting fear.
Looking over my shoulder, wondering what
would happen next as I seek to fulfill my
dreams, praying not to make a mess. I'm
older and still fighting the battle "now even
harder" Oh Lord what is wrong?
I am a lot more mature and that's a good
thing because as I grow more, success is
what my life will bring. So to that
everlasting fear, good-by forever.
I'm taking over now and my future shows
much brighter weather.

## “My baby girl”

My baby girl means everything to me But when she grows up, I will have to set her free. In my heart she will always remain because the love that we share will never change. She keeps me going when I am down and when I discipline her even though she frowns, she’s a very happy child and for that I am grateful. She’s always laughing and extremely playful. I’m not trying to brag. I’m just a happy mother proud of my baby girl, the best little girl in the world.

## "To my Pastor"

My self-esteem was so low and all I could do was put my-self down, but my father sent a messenger, much like an angel that helped turn my Spirit around. You taught me how to love myself, to be strong in mind, body and soul. You helped me gain a new outlook on life and that gift is worth more than gold. I keep your words of wisdom close to my heart so on days when I'm feeling down, I can hear your voice full of confidence, It gives my Spirit a new jumpstart. I am grateful for all that you have taught me. Your services are so anointed sounding just like a pep-rally.

Cheering for the Lord of course hearing sounds of praise from the congregation's voice. Thank you Pastor Jamison, I love you so much. Keep teaching the word, my life you have surely touched.

## "To whom it may concern"

My life is changing and I'm growing
Stronger in faith each day, my mind is
conditioned to change and these things are
because of the Lord. I'm happier now than
I've ever been. What the world has to offer
is nothing compared to the way I am now.
I believe in my savior and he believes in me
He keeps me going through thick and thin.
I'm forever grateful for what he has done.
Can you understand what I'm saying?
I know I'm not the only one. I'm not afraid
of facing things in this world anymore. My
heavenly father protects me and carries me
through many open doors. If you can relate
to me don't sit still. Stand on your feet and
praise him because my father is the real deal

## “Stand up and hold your head high”

Stand up and hold your head high

Reach out to him, Believe and receive

the blessings of the Lord, Surrender your

thoughts and all the stress in your life,

Relax your mind and meditate on his Word

God will relieve you and you’ll feel free as a

bird, To fly to the most high places

there’s no limit to what you can do

Stand up and hold your head high

because thy father is with you

## “I’ve finally found my purpose in life”

I’ve finally found my purpose in life. God has revealed to me, my mission to win souls to Christ. When I examine my past and all the trials I went through. It was to strengthen my weaknesses for the job I’m about to do. I no longer put the world before God. He is my life and I plan around him. Anything else, gets done on a whim. I’m on fire for the Lord and he fills my every void. So, I have no need to regret or live in the past. I’ve finally found my purpose in life, finally at last.

## “I have a goal”

I have a goal to be the best woman I can. Telling all of my married sisters to stand by your man. For all of my brothers, respect your woman because with the bond that you share no disaster can take you under. Reach out to our youth in the most positive way, so that when they grow up, life will be o.k. Lecture if you must, but be a good listener. Teach them to be kind to all of God’s children. Tell them not to stab the backs of their sisters and brothers. Teach them the goodness that we were taught by our own mothers. I have a goal to be free of wicked tears. I have a goal to reap the most successful years.

## "I am a female"

I am a female; a woman who was in disguise. I sheltered my deepest feelings until the Holy Spirit opened my eyes. I got married and then divorced. My heart was broken. My self-esteem lost but in the mist of my grief I remembered that Jesus died and paid the cost. I didn't have to feel sorry anymore. I could forgive and began to heal. It was a process that I thought would never end. At times I didn't think I would make it suddenly the Holy Spirit uttered don't give up. These words I will never forget.

## “I won’t give up”

I’m learning to be a child of God and it’s not easy sometimes, but I won’t give up. I’ve never finished much in life but this time, I won’t give up. Satan tries to destroy me, but I won’t give up. My enemies plot against me, still I won’t give up. My father reaches out to save me, so I won’t give up. Please ask for strength when you are about to fall and please don’t give up.

## “To my younger generation”
### (Words of Wisdom)

Be a leader and not a follower. Ask for guidance because you’re the ox not the tail.It is wise to ask for peace within yourself guidance, wisdom, strength, stability loving and forgiving hearts and the ability to help others and care about one’s feelings. Remember to do unto others as you would have others to do unto you. You can be a child of God. Without him, you’re nothing, with him, you’re more than a conqueror. Don’t let the flesh fool you. The world might seem pleasing to the eye but as they say, don’t judge a book by its cover.

Once you choose to get to know the Lord and develop a relationship with him, you have the key to the entire world and there's nothing positive in it you can't do. This is the key to eternity. Open the door to your everlasting life.

## “Words to the wise about temptation”

Every minute and every hour, we are submitted to some type of temptation. We must stay alert and know when we are being tempted. We must be more demanding than satan is, when he is tempting us to do something negative. Be strong and stand on theWord of God. It will give you the strength you need to survive. The reward for obedience can be as great as we want it to be.

## “Leap out on faith”

Is your life not what you hoped it would be?

Leap out, on faith! And you will see

That nothing positive is impossible

Through the eyes of the Lord

No nothing at all

Leap out on faith and make that call

Don’t let anyone get your spirit down

telling you, you will never be anything

and laughing when they see you frown

Leap out on faith and show them who’s the

Boss and if they don’t have faith in you,

oh well then, that’s their lost

## “When you have been blessed”

When you have been blessed, as we all are each day. Don’t be selfish, share it with someone else bow down and help them pray. Caring about others, says a lot. Don’t think you’re better, because you’re not. We are all equal in the eyes of the Lord and we are all special. Now that’s a great reward.

## “Wings of faith”

I was afraid and now I’m not. I cried, I stumbled and prayed a lot. I’ve made so many unstable choices. What I thought would hold up on a shaky foundation crumbled to pieces. I was afraid that my hopes and dreams were too far for me to reach. Through all my trials and tribulations all I could do was doubt. The next thing I knew, I was hanging on a wing and a prayer. As soon as I opened up my heart to Jesus he assured me that he would always be there. Now I stand strong with two wings and many answered prayers.

I humbled myself and faced my fears after humiliation and many tears. I can assure you that it was God's grace and mercy that brought me here. To a solid foundation where I stand wearing wings of faith.

www.ingramcontent.com/pod-product-compliance
Lightning Source LLC
LaVergne TN
LVHW020635100826
845148LV00012B/2186

* 9 7 8 0 9 8 1 6 5 0 9 0 6 *